Haunted Houses

New and future titles in the series include:
The Bermuda Triangle
The Curse of King Tut
The Extinction of the Dinosaurs
Haunted Houses
UFOs
Vampires
Witches

The Mystery Library

Haunted Houses

Patricia D. Netzley

Lucent Books, Inc.
P.O. Box 289011, San Diego, California

For Matthew, Sarah, and Jacob

Library of Congress Cataloging-in-Publication Data

Netzley, Patricia D.
  Haunted houses / by Patricia D. Netzley.
    p. cm. — (The Mystery library)
  Includes bibliographical references and index.
    ISBN 1-56006-685-7 (alk. paper)
    Summary: Discusses haunted houses including ghosts and
apparitions, poltergeists, communicating with spirits, and
investigating hauntings.
    1. Ghosts. 2. Poltergeists. 3. Haunted houses. I. Title II.
Mystery library (Lucent Books)
  BF 1461.N48 2000
  133.1—dc21
                                            00-008129

Printed in the U.S.A.

Contents

Foreword

In Shakespeare's immortal play *Hamlet*, the young Danish aristocrat Horatio has clearly been astonished and disconcerted by his encounter with a ghost-like apparition on the castle battlements. "There are more things in heaven and earth," his friend Hamlet assures him, "than are dreamt of in your philosophy."

Many people today would readily agree with Hamlet that the world and the vast universe surrounding it are teeming with wonders and oddities that remain largely outside the realm of present human knowledge or understanding. How did the universe begin? What caused the dinosaurs to become extinct? Was the lost continent of Atlantis a real place or merely legendary? Does a monstrous creature lurk beneath the surface of Scotland's Loch Ness? These are only a few of the intriguing questions that remain unanswered, despite the many great strides made by science in recent centuries.

Lucent Books' Mystery Library series is dedicated to exploring these and other perplexing, sometimes bizarre, and often disturbing or frightening wonders. Each volume in the series presents the best-known tales, incidents, and evidence surrounding the topic in question. Also included are the opinions and theories of scientists and other experts who have attempted to unravel and solve the ongoing mystery. And supplementing this information is a fulsome list of sources for further reading, providing the reader with the means to pursue the topic further.

The Mystery Library will satisfy every young reader's fascination for the unexplained. As one of history's greatest scientists, physicist Albert Einstein, put it:

"The most beautiful thing we can experience is the mysterious. It is the source of all true art and science. He to whom this emotion is a stranger, who can no longer wonder and stand rapt in awe, is as good as dead: his eyes are closed."

Introduction

Mysterious Sights, Sounds, and Smells

Every year thousands of tourists travel to San Jose, California, to visit a 160-room mansion known as the Winchester House. Some people are attracted by the building's unusual architecture, which features secret passages to hidden rooms, windows backed by solid walls, and staircases that go nowhere. Others are drawn by rumors that the house is haunted—repeatedly being visited by the spirit of someone long dead.

No one knows the identity of this spirit, although many suspect that it is the original owner of the house, Sarah Winchester, who began construction on her mansion in 1884 and continued adding rooms until her death in 1922. Her compulsive building was based on her own belief in spirits. As the daughter-in-law of the man who invented the Winchester rifle, she became convinced that her construction projects would in some way appease the ghosts of those killed by the rifle and that if she did not appease them she would die. Throughout her life she tried to contact the spirits through a ritual known as a séance, and she incorporated the number thirteen into her building projects because she thought it would appeal to ghosts. Some of her stairways, for example, have thirteen steps, and her chandeliers have thirteen lights. There are thirteen bathrooms in the house, and one room has thirteen windows.

Today many people wonder whether Sarah Winchester's house has indeed become appealing to spirits. In the years since her death, visitors to the mansion have reported hearing mysterious footsteps and slamming doors. A tour guide heard his name whispered in a room where no one else was present, and a caretaker heard breathing behind him when he was alone. Other people have felt cold spots in an otherwise warm room and smelled soup cooking in a kitchen devoid of pots.

These incidents, which all involve the senses of the person experiencing them, exemplify the most common characteristic

Cold spots, unexplainably unlocked doors, and mysterious footsteps at Sarah Winchester's mansion in San Jose, California, lead some people to believe that the house is haunted.

of houses said to be haunted: mysterious yet recognizable noises and/or odors. Another characteristic, though somewhat less common, is an unexplained physical change in the house. For example, Allen Weitzel, a director of food and merchandising at Winchester House, has reported finding locked doors inexplicably unlocked and lights spontaneously turned off and on. One morning he found his office soaked with water. In their book *Historic Haunted America*, Michael Norman and Beth Scott report: "Everything from the paperwork on his desk to his chair and the floor was sopping wet. Even a pencil holder was filled with water. A light rain had fallen overnight, but not nearly enough to cause the extent of damage Weitzel found. And, most intriguing of all, the ceiling and walls were completely dry."[1]

Many other reports of haunted houses feature the unexplained opening of doors and windows and the rearrangement of furniture and pictures, sometimes while an observer is present but more often when no one is looking. When people are present such movements often appear to be made by an invisible hand, but in some cases a ghost appears to be moving the object.

Modern researchers define a ghost as the image of a person, animal, or thing that appears regularly but unexplainably in a particular place. For example, there are several stories about ghost trains that pass along a particular stretch of railroad track on the anniversary of a train wreck. In the case of the Winchester House, in the years since Sarah Winchester's death, a few visitors have claimed to have seen the image of a woman who looks like her in certain parts of the house.

Similar ghost sightings have been reported throughout history and throughout the world. Beginning in the late nineteenth century, they have triggered scientific investigations into haunted houses, along with attempts by nonscientists to contact spirits. Both scientists and laypeople have sought to investigate ghost stories and determine what might be causing the strange events associated with them. Some researchers have concluded that living people—not spirits—are responsible for the phenomena, but others believe that ghosts really can affect the physical world.

Public opinion polls indicate that approximately 25 percent of Americans believe that ghosts really can haunt a house, and roughly 67 percent believe in life after death. In one 1984 survey conducted by the University of Chicago's National Opinion Research Center, 42 percent of Americans said that they had personally been in touch with someone who had died. In a 1987 Epcot Center poll, 13 percent of participants said that they had actually seen a ghost.

Ghost sightings have been reported throughout history and the world.

Of the people who do not believe in ghosts, some argue that a person's soul ceases to exist when the body dies while others say that the soul survives the body's death but cannot later return to the world of the living in any form. But if there are no ghosts, what would explain the phenomena associated with haunted houses? These phenomena have been widely experienced, and as Jerome Clark points out in his book *Unexplained!*, even if scientists were to prove that ghosts do not exist, they would still have to provide an explanation for what people take to be ghost sightings:

> To say that you have "seen" [a strange being] is not necessarily to say that the anomaly lives on in the world when it is not briefly occupying your vision and scaring the daylights out of you. We may experience unbelievable things, but our experiences of them may tell us nothing about them except that they can be

experienced. You can "see" a mermaid or a werewolf, but however impressive the experience may be to you, the rest of us cannot infer from that that mermaids and werewolves are "real." In fact, we can be certain that they are not. And that is all we can be certain of, because all we have done . . . is to remove one explanation (that mermaids and werewolves live in the world) from consideration while failing to put another in its place.[2]

Therefore, even scientists who do not believe in ghosts seek to examine haunted houses and develop theories related to the phenomena that people encounter in such places. Meanwhile, those who do believe in ghosts work to find indisputable evidence not only that the spirit survives death but also that it is able to interact with the living.

Chapter 1

Ghosts and Apparitions

In 1953 several magazines featured a story of an unusual phenomenon in Greenwich Village, New York. Residents of a studio apartment building located at 51 West Tenth Street claimed that for several years they had been seeing the ghost of artist John La Farge, who died in 1910.

The ghost of John La Farge, an American artist and writer, was rumored to haunt the New York apartment building where he once had his studio.

The first sighting of La Farge occurred in 1944 in a part of the building that was once the artist's studio. A couple living there, Mr. and Mrs. Feodor Rimsky, returned home from the theater to find a man standing behind one of their chairs. When Mr. Rimsky approached the man, the figure vanished. Later the Rimskys saw a picture of La Farge and recognized him as the man they had seen vanish. From that point on, they often heard strange noises, and in 1947 a guest to their apartment—who knew nothing of La Farge's previous appearance— saw the man again.

The following year La Farge began materializing in a neighboring studio, that of illustrator John Alan Maxwell. Subsequent tenants also saw La Farge, who often opened and closed drawers and was sometimes accompanied by an image that looked like his wife. The artist's ghostly visitations continued until the building was torn down in 1956.

Crisis Apparitions

La Farge's repeated appearances qualify him as a ghost. Some people also use the term *haunting apparition* to describe such an image because a ghost is a type of apparition. However, there are so many things about a ghost that are different from other apparitions that many reject this term.

Apparitions are solid figures that sometimes seem so real they cast shadows or show their reflections in mirrors.

Apparitions are images of people, places, or things that are not really present but are typically perceived as solid, realistic figures rather than transparent ones. In fact, on occasion they appear so real that they seem to cast shadows and/or have reflections in mirrors, although they might also appear to walk through solid objects or vanish. However, whereas an apparition can represent a living person who is merely some distance away, a ghost of a person always represents someone who has died or an object that no longer exists. Moreover, whereas a ghost can reappear for years, apparitions are usually of short duration.

In fact, the most common type of apparition appears only once. Called a crisis apparition, it occurs when a living person is sick, seriously injured, or otherwise in crisis. One example of such an apparition was reported by Mrs. John Church, an American who saw the image of her brother while visiting Asia. As Mrs. Church recalls,

> One night I awoke from a sound sleep on hearing my brother, David, call my name. At the time he was living in Goshen, New York, where he operated a charter air service. Opening my eyes, I found him standing a few feet away. . . . I noted that he was wearing his pilot's uniform. Curiously, though, his face was blank, lacking any features. Checking to make sure I was awake and not dreaming, I pinched myself, identified my surroundings, and touched my husband at my side. All the time I stared at my brother; there was no doubt about it — he was there in the room. . . . After a moment or two his figure wavered, and then it slowly dissolved into vapor. . . . Upon my return to the States a year later, I related my experience to my brother. He recalled a terrifying flight the previous year when he thought he was going to die; both engines of his twin-engine aircraft had failed, but as the plane plunged, one engine miraculously started up again. Although we were unable to synchronize the two experiences exactly, we found they had occurred very close in time.[3]

Crisis apparitions can also represent people who have just died or are about to die. One of the most famous examples of such an apparition occurred in December 1918 when an eighteen-year-old British pilot named David McConnell died in a plane crash. At the moment of his death—at 3:25 P.M. as indicated by his smashed watch—his roommate, a man named Larkin, had heard footsteps outside his room. When the door opened, he saw McConnell walk in and greet him. Larkin then asked McConnell how his flight was, and McConnell replied that he had had a good trip, then left.

Approximately one-half hour later, Larkin told another person that he had just talked to McConnell; from this conversation, investigators eventually determined that Larkin had seen his roommate sometime between 3:15 and 3:30 P.M.

When Larkin heard about McConnell's death, he was sure there had been some mistake about the time. He could not believe that the person he had seen had been an apparition. It took him two weeks to accept this explanation, whereupon he wrote a detailed account of his experience that, coupled with testimony from those he spoke to around the time of the event, makes the McConnell incident one of the best-documented crisis apparitions. However, since there is no objective proof of what Larkin saw, some people believe he simply mistook another pilot for McConnell or only imagined seeing his roommate.

In either case, no one ever saw an apparition of McConnell again. Crisis apparitions rarely recur, and there is usually a close personal relationship between the person in crisis and the person seeing the vision, the latter of which is called the experient (one who is experiencing the event) or less commonly the percipient (one who is perceiving the event). Other types of apparitions that are also typically short-lived phenomena include visions of deceased relatives that appear to experients who are themselves near death as well as apparitions that deliver a warning or other message.

Trying to Communicate

In the case of the latter, stories abound about apparitions who revealed the location of hidden money or important documents or offered warnings that saved another person's life. Apparitions have told sailors to steer a different course, asked pilots to check for mechanical problems on their planes before taking off, and in the case of murder victims, provided information that led to the capture of their killer. Apparitions usually continue to appear until their messages have been acted on, whereupon they are never seen again.

Such was the case in one of the earliest written accounts of an apparition. It was described in the letters of Pliny the Younger, a statesman who lived in ancient Rome from approximately A.D. 62 to 113. Pliny mentions a house in Athens in which the apparition of an old man shackled in long chains regularly appeared. Sometimes visitors to the house would only hear the chains rattling, but others would see the ghost itself. One day, according to Pliny, the apparition led a visitor to a spot in the garden. When the spot was excavated, the bones of a human being bound in chains were found. Once these bones were buried with appropriate religious rites, the apparition was never seen by anyone again.

This example illustrates another defining difference between ghosts and other types of apparitions. Nonhaunting apparitions—whether of the living or the dead—appear to know that they are being watched and might try to communicate with the experient. They also seem aware of their surroundings and might move around a chair, for example, in order to touch a particular object on a table. In contrast, ghosts typically seem oblivious to their surroundings and will often repeat the same actions over and over regardless of what objects are in a room or who is watching. Moreover, experients watching a ghost rarely report that it tries to communicate with them.

For example, at the Harbour Oaks Inn in Pass Christian, Mississippi, people who have spent the night in one particular room sometimes report seeing a "ghost girl" who continually picks up ghostly toys and sewing items and puts them on a table. The ghost seems unaware of the hotel guests,

Apparitions tend to appear until the messages they hope to convey are understood. Once they have accomplished this goal, they typically vanish and are not seen again.

although some say that they are affected by her. One of the hotel proprietors, Diane Brugger, explains: "The 'feelings' associated with her are very compassionate: cheerful, playful, helpful, warm, and nonthreatening. Those who have experienced her feel a sense of loss when she leaves."[4]

Ties to a Place

The ghost girl only appears in one part of the hotel. This is another common characteristic of ghosts: They are seen only in one general area. In most cases, the place they haunt is somehow related to the death of the person they have been identified as representing. For example, the spirit of a person might appear to be haunting a place related to that person's work, as was the case with the artist La Farge, or a place related to his or her death, which is by far the most typical type of haunting connection.

One example of several spirits appearing to haunt their place of death involves the Westover Plantation near Charles City, Virginia. Built in 1726, the plantation house was once the home of William Byrd II, who helped found the city of Richmond, Virginia. Byrd had a daughter named Evelyn who became a recluse after her father refused to allow her to marry the man she loved. Her depression led to poor health, and she died at home in 1737 when she was only twenty-nine years old. From that time on, many people claimed they had seen Evelyn's ghost in and around her house. Dressed in a white dress, she performed ordinary actions like brushing her hair or walking across a lawn. Sometimes she seemed oblivious to the people viewing her, but other times she seemed to look directly at them.

In subsequent years two other ghosts were also seen at Westover Plantation. One of them was Evelyn's sister-in-law Elizabeth Hill Carter Byrd, who was crushed to death in her bedroom when a heavy trunk fell on her. The other was William Byrd III, Elizabeth's husband, who

committed suicide in the house after incurring heavy gambling debts. But despite their untimely deaths—another common aspect of many ghost stories—these spirits did not seem to observers to be upset or violent. Instead, as with the ghost girl, they were largely oblivious to their surroundings.

The Westover Plantation in Virginia is reportedly home to several spirits of people who met their untimely deaths there.

Other ghosts, however, can appear to be agitated. For instance, in 1910 a family in St. Paul, Minnesota, saw a dark-haired, mustached man in an overcoat climbing the stairs up from the cellar of their house. Frightened, they shut the cellar door before he could reach the top; but later, when they opened it again, the cellar was empty. A short time after this, the woman of the house, Hattie Sebastian, and two of her friends saw the man again. She subsequently told a newspaper reporter that it was a terrible experience. . . . He wore a hairy overcoat and a pair of moccasins. A black mustache hid his upper lip and I distinctly remember that he had brown eyes. . . . He seemed to move toward me until, just as I felt his arms were about to clasp me about the neck, the lower part of his body faded away. Slowly, while I stood terror-stricken, the other part disappeared.[5]

Sebastian saw the man yet again a few days later, and after speaking with the newspaper reporter, her house became famous. Its fame increased after Sebastian discovered bone fragments, crucifixes, and rosaries buried in the dirt floor of her cellar, along with a letter written in French. Fearing the letter had some kind of evil incantations on it, she burned it but turned the bone fragments over to the police, who in turn gave them to experts at the University of Minnesota for examination. However, the bones were too deteriorated to determine whether they were human or animal. Nonetheless, Sebastian and her family decided to move away from the house, which then stood empty. Meanwhile, no one could determine the ghost's identity, although someone whose family had previously owned the house said the description of the man was similar to that of a Frenchman who had once rented the place.

Spirit Photographs

Sebastian and her friends were accused of having overactive imaginations that had led them to hallucinate. This is a common accusation made whenever someone claims to have seen anything paranormal. However, some evidence seems to support the view that ghosts and other apparitions are hallucinations.

Although these images typically appear solid, they in fact have the transparency of an illusion; experients can put their hands through them. In addition, apparitions leave behind no physical evidence, such as footprints, that indicate they interacted with their environment, and often an object that the experient thought was moved by the apparition turns out not to have been. Perhaps more importantly, when a group of people are involved in an apparition sighting, not everyone present can see the image. This suggests that the event is a figment of the experient's imagination.

The inability to obtain a photograph of a ghost is also an indication that the experience might be in the experient's mind. Although many supposed photographs of ghosts have been produced over the years, none has been proven to be genuine. Some have been obvious fakes while others are clearly the result of errors in the photographic process. Only a few warrant closer examination.

The first purported spirit photograph was made in Boston in 1862, when a professional photographer named Mumler displayed a self-portrait that had a ghostly image in the background. This image resembled Mumler's cousin, who had died twelve years earlier. Mumler then claimed that he knew how to take pictures of other people's dead relatives as well. He set up a thriving business in spirit photography, but he had to leave Boston when some of his background "spirit" images were recognized as Mumler's employees in various costumes. Mumler later resurfaced in New York, where he was eventually accused of fraud and put on trial. His case was dismissed when several of his former clients stepped forward to defend his work as legitimate. The witnesses remained certain that they had seen the spirits of their loved ones.

Nonetheless, Mumler lived in a time when still photographers were well aware of a technique called the double exposure. In this technique, the photographer takes one picture on top of another using the same photographic plate, thereby putting two images—photographed separately— together in the same picture. Mumler could easily have taken a picture of a "spirit" prior to his client's sitting, then photographed his client on the same piece of film. Other so-called spirit photographers from the period used a similar method to put the figure of a famous deceased person into their pictures. They would cut out the face from a photograph of Abraham Lincoln or some other historical figure, place it on a background, and photograph it as part of a double exposure.

Another way to create a false spirit was to use a dummy. One spirit photographer named Buget, who

Spirit photographers were popular in the late nineteenth century. These men had many supporters, but none of their photographs ever proved to be genuine.

worked in both Paris and London during the 1870s, employed a dummy whose head could be replaced. With a wide variety of heads to choose from, he was able to closely approximate the appearance of the deceased, based on details his clients unwittingly revealed about their loved ones. But just as with Mumler, when Buget was arrested for fraud and put on trial in 1875, his clients refused to believe they had been tricked—even though Buget had confessed to the crime. They thought his confession had been coerced, and even when shown the dummy, they still denied that it could possibly have been used to make the images in the spirit photographs they had purchased.

Subjective Analysis

But with the advent of movie special effects in the 1890s, people became less trusting of the photographic images they saw. During this period a filmmaker named George Melies produced dozens of short movies that featured multiple exposures, including *The One Man Band* (1900), which allowed him to play seven different roles in one scene. Consequently, spirit photographers went out of fashion. However, images of spirits that were apparently photographed accidentally continued to excite the public.

Most of these images were caused by the crude photographic processes of the early twentieth century. For example, in 1891 Sybell Corbet took a photograph of an empty room and later discovered a ghostly figure sitting in a chair. However, in order to take the picture, the film was exposed for an hour while the camera was left unattended. This meant that someone could have entered the room, sat in the chair, then left while the picture was being taken, thereby creating the ghost image. Many other accidental "ghost photographs" of the late nineteenth and early twentieth centuries were caused by errors in the developing process that produced strange lights or blurs. Cracks in the camera casing, which enabled light to leak in during the photographic process, could also cause the strange effects.

Occasionally, though, a photograph has captured a ghostly image that photographic experts cannot explain. For instance, in 1959 Mabel Chinnery of England took a photograph of her husband sitting alone in his car. When the photograph was developed, she saw a ghostly image sitting in the back seat. She was certain the image was that of her mother, who had recently died. A photographic expert later declared that this image could not have been created by any kind of double exposure or reflection of light. Similarly, in 1966 clergyman Ralph Hardy of Canada took a photograph in a British maritime museum and later noticed the image of a hooded figure on a staircase. Again, an expert declared that no photographic trick could have accounted for the image.

Hans Holzer, a parapsychologist, or expert in the psychology of paranormal phenomena, has examined many spirit photographs and believes some to be genuine. But Holzer is frustrated over skeptics' refusal to accept such evidence as proof that ghosts exist:

> Despite the overwhelming evidence that these photographs were genuine—in almost all cases even the motive for fraud was totally absent—some researchers . . . [continue to promote] the possibility that the results were nothing but fraudulently manufactured double exposures. . . . Prejudice against anything involving a major shift in one's thinking, philosophy of life, and general training is much stronger than we dare admit to ourselves sometimes. . . . We still don't know *all* of the conditions that make these extraordinary photographs

Some photographs, such as this one taken in England in 1936, are difficult to confirm as fakes.

possible and, until we do, obtaining them will be a hit-and-miss affair at best. But the fact that genuine photographs of what are commonly called ghosts have been taken by a number of people, under conditions excluding fraud or faulty equipment, of course, is food for serious thought.[6]

Skeptics, however, point out that just because an expert cannot detect trickery does not mean that it was not employed. They also argue that people see what they want to see when they look at a "ghostly" image. In discussing a spirit photograph produced by Antonetta Petrignani in the 1980s, magician James Randi, who established an organization for skeptics called the Committee for the Scientific Investigation of Claims of the Paranormal, says:

> This little lady . . . was honestly deceived by her inability to take good pictures. This became sadly evident to me when I examined a huge stack of several hundred Polaroid photos she brought with her and listened to her interpretations of what she saw therein. One of them showed—to her eyes, at least —a man crouching on a plank with a rock beneath it. I could see nothing but a blur of gray and white against a black background. . . . During my examination of her results, I turned the man-on-a-plank shot 180 degrees and submitted it to her again as if I'd selected it from among the unsorted photos. This time, viewing it upside down, she said she saw part of an old building and a dog in the photo. Further examination showed that of her twelve most successful shots . . . six were viewed upside down, two had been turned 90 degrees to the left, two others had been rotated 90 degrees to the right, and two were right side up.[7]

In other words, Petrignani had unconsciously turned the pictures until she was able to discern an image, the image she discerned was based on her imagination, and others could not objectively identify the same image. This is true in other cases of ghost photographs. Not everyone looking at the photograph will see the same image—unless someone first tells him or her what to look for.

Imagination and Telepathy

Because of experients like Petrignani, as well as the fact that no indisputable photographic evidence of ghosts currently exists, most parapsychologists believe that all ghost sightings are created by the experient. Yet, they dispute whether these images are the product of simple imagination. Some scientists propose that they might instead be the result of mental telepathy, the ability of one person to send a thought or image to another person's mind in real time.

Various theories that attribute ghost sightings to telepathy have been developed over the years. Some people have argued that the spirit of a dead person can send its own image telepathically, in real time, to experients from beyond the grave. Others have suggested that telepathic messages from the deceased might have been left behind in

Madame Jumel, wife of Aaron Burr, is rumored to appear on the front balcony of the Jumel Mansion (pictured). Eleanor Sedgewick's theories about telepathy may explain the connection between old houses and ghosts.

a particular place while that person was alive, to be passed on to other minds in later years. For example, Eleanor Sedgewick, a mathematician who began studying hauntings in the late nineteenth century, suggested that a house might be able to absorb telepathic images and messages from people who lived there—images and messages that would later be received by visitors receptive to telepathic communication. This would be one possible explanation of why very old houses inhabited for generations are more likely to have one or more ghosts associated with them. It might also explain the phenomenon of veridical apparitions, which are apparitions that offer some piece of truthful information to the experient that the experient could not have known otherwise.

Under another variation of the telepathic theory, the experient is thought to be projecting an image telepathically into the environment. In other words, the experient's mind is creating the image as an external phenomenon in such a way that it can be visible to others in the same room. This would account for the fact that groups of people visiting a haunted house sometimes see the same image, a phenomenon called a collective apparition. Another theory related to collective apparitions is that one experient—or perhaps the ghost itself—is telepathically transmitting such images into the minds of everyone else present, as opposed to creating it as an external phenomenon. This would explain why some individuals involved in a collective apparition sighting fail to see the ghost; perhaps such individuals are unable to receive telepathic images.

However, there are some problems with the idea that a collective apparition is created telepathically in the minds of those present. First, although all experients participating in a collective viewing see the same apparition, they do not always see it from the same perspective. Some people might see it from the front while others see it from the back or in profile. If a single image is being transmitted to all viewers, one would assume that the appearance of the image would be uniform. Second, animals sometimes appear to see a collective apparition, growling or snapping while others are witnessing the ghost, and there is no conclusive evidence of telepathic ability in animals; in fact, telepathic ability in humans has not even been proven conclusively. Third, if ghosts and apparitions are being caused by telepathy, then how is it that images that appear to be moved by the ghost during its appearance are sometimes found to be moved after the event?

Such was the case at a Tucson, Arizona, high school where a janitor died suddenly of a heart attack in the 1970s. From that point on, school workers after hours saw an apparition of the man, and on several occasions they saw him moving trash cans that were subsequently found to have indeed moved. Cleaning supplies were also found out of place, as though he had taken them to do his work. Skeptics, however, believe that such events were the result of student pranks or employees with active imaginations.

In some cases, though, such spontaneous movements are much harder to dismiss. They are so extreme, so violent, and so obvious to multiple witnesses that there is no way someone could have rigged them to occur. Telepathy cannot explain such movements, so other theories related to mental ability have been proposed instead. Meanwhile, skeptics continue to insist that all events related to ghosts or apparitions must somehow be caused by the experient who reports the event.

Chapter 2

Poltergeists

Between 1817 and 1820, John Bell and his family were tormented by a paranormal phenomenon on their farm near Adams, Tennessee. There are many variations of the story of what happened to the Bell family, but all of these stories share certain features. First, the ghost of an old woman appeared to family members as well as to several people outside the family. Second, the ghost spoke to people and revealed its identity on several occasions. Although the name it gave varied, its most consistent claim was that it was a witch called Kate, and it consequently became known as the Bell Witch. Third, the ghost swore to torment John Bell to death, and from that point on some invisible force pinched, pushed, and otherwise tormented him physically.

This same force also knocked pictures off walls, flipped over chairs, threw dishes and rocks, pulled hair, and tugged blankets off of beds; sometimes these activities were accompanied by piercing shrieks or loud moans. Moreover, these violent activities took place in front of many witnesses. In fact, after national newspapers reported on the ghost's antics, the Bell farm became somewhat of a tourist attraction, with people coming from as far away as New York to see the phenomenon.

Violent Spirits

Hauntings that involve such extreme and violent movements are said to be caused by a poltergeist, a term that comes from the German words *poltern*, meaning "noisy," and *geist*, meaning "spirit." Poltergeists are spirits that seem intent on causing trouble. As with the Bell Witch, they make loud noises, move objects around, and can push, pinch, and shove experients. They might also cause spontaneous, unexplainable fires and are often connected to strange incidents related to water, such as the appearance in a room of puddles with no apparent cause.

Poltergeists are generally violent, angry spirits who seem determined to cause trouble.

Poltergeists are distinguished from ghosts, which might also cause unexplained sounds and movements, by their violent nature. In addition, poltergeists differ from ghosts in that poltergeist phenomena often occur during the day whereas most other haunting phenomena usually occur at night. Poltergeist behavior can start suddenly and end suddenly—after months or years—and it is not always accompanied by the presence of an apparition. When there is an apparition, it is often difficult for experients to associate it with a specific deceased person.

As with the Bell Witch, some poltergeists remain confined to a particular place. However, many haunt not a house but a person, following a specific individual around for days or even weeks. As an example, in his book *Introduction to Parapsychology*, H. J. Irwin reports that

> in mid-1965 unexplained movements of merchandise occurred in the chinaware department of a Bremen [Germany] store. Investigations by police and other authorities failed to establish any normal explanation for the events but they evidently were connected in some obscure way with a 15-year-old apprentice employee in the department. The lad was dismissed and the disturbances in the store immediately came to an end. The young man subsequently obtained a job as an apprentice in a Freiburg [Germany] electrical shop. In March 1966 he was asked to drill holes in a concrete wall and to install wall hooks. The task was done properly but a little later it was found that the hooks came loose in the presence of the young apprentice. He was accused of being to blame. In a test of this a freshly attached hook was observed to come loose within two minutes while the apprentice stood about a yard . . . from the wall.[8]

Troubled Adolescents

In studying incidents where poltergeists seemed to haunt one particular person, investigators have found that many of the experients involved in such situations were emotionally troubled adolescents. In one study approximately 62 percent of experients were under age eighteen and living away from home when the poltergeist activities began. Interestingly, the Bell Witch case also involved an adolescent. During the time of the haunting, Bell had nine children, one of whom was his twelve-year-old daughter, Betsy. Betsy was the first person to see the ghost of the Bell Witch, and although the witch tormented her father and other family members, it left her alone. Once Betsy became engaged to be married, however, the ghost began to torment her as well. It only stopped its poltergeist activity after John Bell fell into a mysterious coma and died.

Because poltergeist behavior is usually associated with a particular person, some experts in the paranormal theorize that such behavior must somehow be caused by that person. Thus, some of these experts believe that the term *poltergeist* should not be used to define the behavior at all. For example, parapsychologist William G. Roll says that it is wrong to use a word that means "noisy spirit" because "it implies an agency apart from any living organism." Roll believes that poltergeists are instead a "person-centered phenomenon"[9] caused by something known as recurrent spontaneous psychokinesis (RSPK).

Psychokinesis (PK) is a type of psychic ability that enables the experient to move or bend objects at will; RSPK is this same ability performed spontaneously and repeatedly. Skeptics have attributed all documented incidents of PK to trickery, and they do not believe that RSPK is any more real. However, parapsychologists suggest that poltergeist experients' unconscious minds might be using RSPK as a way to relieve emotional tension. H. J. Irwin argues that this theory is supported by the fact that most poltergeist activity occurs in the presence of an emotionally troubled teenager because "it suggests that poltergeist disturbances in some way are associated with emotional conflict in the focal person. The frequency of adolescent cases may indicate further that the [experient] is not in a position to express the conflict openly."[10]

In studying PK and RSPK, researchers have developed several ways to test an experient's ability to move objects without conscious effort. One of the most common methods is to have the experient roll dice, typically using an electric dice-tumbling machine rather than the hands, with the goal of making the dice show certain

Here, a teenage boy cleans up after a poltergeist disturbance. Paranormal experts often connect poltergeist activity with troubled teenagers.

numerical combinations. People associated with incidents of RSPK typically roll the correct numbers at a rate higher than is dictated by chance, but skeptics do not accept this as proof that PK exists.

The House-Proud Poltergeist

The RSPK theory also does not seem to apply to poltergeist behavior that is not centered around an "emotionally charged" person and is apparently associated with a place rather than a person. One example of such a haunting was mentioned in a 1984 *Journal of Psychical Research* article on the case of "Frances Freeborn" (a pseudonym, as were other names in the article). Immediately after purchasing a home in Bakersfield, California, in 1981, Freeborn began noticing some unusual events. While she was moving into the home, she heard loud noises that seemed to have no source. When she woke up in the morning she often discovered that doors and cabinets that had been left closed had opened during the night. In addition, lights that she had turned off before leaving the house would be turned on when she returned. She hired carpenters and electricians to check the cabinets, doors, and lights, but no one could find any reason for what was happening.

Then one day an event occurred that led Freeborn to decide that a spirit was responsible for her problems. She hung an old picture on a wall, left the room, and later found it on the floor. She hung it again, this time more solidly. Again, she later found it on the floor. She tried hanging it someplace else, but the same thing occurred. After trying four other spots, she finally got it to stay on the wall. Her successful attempt was preceded by an odd feeling that the spot was the only place the picture belonged.

A few days later Freeborn was visited by the man who had sold her the house, "Luke Cowley." His mother-in-law, "Meg Lyons," had died there, after which the house had stood vacant for five years with all of her belongings in tact. In fact, very little had been removed from the house until Freeborn took possession of it, and Freeborn had retained much of Lyons' furniture. When Cowley noticed the previously troublesome picture hanging on the wall, he blanched. The picture looked very similar to one his mother once had, and she had hung it in the exact place.

Freeborn subsequently realized that whenever she tried to change anything about the surroundings, a strange feeling of uneasiness came over her. She began to wonder whether the spirit of Meg Lyons was in the house, and she felt that her suspicion was confirmed once she began a bedroom redecorating project in January 1982. As soon as she brought her paint, wallpaper, and other redecorating materials in the house, she experienced a sense of foreboding, and before she could begin the project, some dramatic poltergeist behavior began. She heard loud banging, saw windows and doors slam open and shut, and felt something shove her. She fled the house determined to sell it.

Once Freeborn left the house, she experienced no other poltergeist phenomena. She also had no previous history of experiencing poltergeist phenomena, and in fact apparently did not even believe in ghosts prior to buying the Lyons house. Only after normal explanations for the events were exhausted did she consult experts in the paranormal.

Ground Settling

However, skeptics point out that Freeborn did not actually consider all other possibilities. After she developed her conviction that Lyons was in the house, she attributed all strange behavior to the spirit world. She did not, however, consider the fact that her moving doors and pictures, as well as various noises, might be attributed to the fact that the foundation of a house can sometimes move and shift due to a process called ground settling. A. R. G. Owen explains how this process might relate to hauntings in his book *Can We Explain the Poltergeist?*:

> A sudden movement of the fabric of a house may "jar" a clock and cause it to stop. Underground hydraulic pressure tilts the floor slowly, until it suddenly returns to its former level on release of the pressure. If this cycle is repeated a heavy piece of

Shifts in a house's foundation or pressure underground is called ground settling. Skeptics argue that ground settling, not ghosts, is responsible for poltergeist activity.

furniture will advance over the floor in a series of "steps." Chairs having an uneven weight distribution are particularly likely to travel in this way. If the floor is vibrating up and down it will cause chairs to jump up and down. . . . When a whole house is tilted and dropped back into position some of the walls are tilted from the vertical and then return to it suddenly. If the displacement is large enough, articles will fall from shelves or mantlepiece. If the house has a wooden frame this will be elastic and articles may be "thrown" into the room from opposite directions. . . . When people feel themselves pushed by an invisible power towards some part of the room, it is the room that is moving towards them, and they invent the invisible power to account for lurches for which they know they are not responsible.[11]

Conflicting stories explain the haunting of the Borley Rectory in England. However, most paranormal experts agree that the building is haunted by the spirit of a nun who once lived there.

Skeptics often blame ground settling for "poltergeist" behavior connected to a particular house, and in some instances the shifting of the earth has indeed been proven to be the cause. For example, in Ousedale, England, in 1955, paranormal investigator Trevor H. Hall examined a poltergeist case in a house being used as a medical clinic. The behavior of the "poltergeist" was fairly mild; the doctors regularly heard unexplained loud noises but only occasionally did objects appear to move. In an attempt to explain the noises, the doctors first called in a variety of building experts; but when nothing could be found wrong with the structure of the house, they called Hall.

Hall quickly determined that the regularity of the noises fit a certain pattern, and he set out to find out what might be happening at the same time each day to cause them. Noting that the house sat near the mouth of a river, he determined that the noises were loudest when the tides were high and did not occur at all when the tides were low. Consequently, he concluded that the ground was in some way shifting in accordance with the increase and decrease in the river's water level. Although he did not prove that this was the cause of the strange activity, his timetable convinced the doctors that no spirit was haunting their house.

The Borley Rectory

Sometimes, however, it is more difficult to ascribe place-associated poltergeist behavior to ground settling. Such is the case with the haunting of the Borley Rectory, located just northeast of London, England. Built in 1863 on the site of an old manor, the building was first inhabited by the Reverend Henry Bull, then by his son Harry. From the outset, the Bull family believed the structure to be haunted by the spirit of a nun. Several family members saw this apparition on many occasions, both at night and during the day, and in one case four people witnessed the apparition at the same time. In addition, many people heard unexplained footsteps, whispers, and other mysterious noises in the house.

In 1929 Harry Price—one of the first people to investigate paranormal phenomena using scientific methodology—became interested in the house and began a long-term study of the site. The following year the house became the scene of violent poltergeist activity that included incidents of stone throwing. People would find themselves pelted with rocks for no apparent reason and from no apparent source.

Stone throwing is a very common characteristic of a poltergeist experience. Rocks seem to appear out of nowhere, and they might change direction abruptly while traveling. It is also common to see rocks falling from the sky—or even from a ceiling.

Fascinated by such phenomena, Price took up residence in the Borley Rectory from 1937 to 1938 so that he could investigate it more thoroughly. Along with a team of researchers, he took detailed notes, measured the distances that objects traveled, and tried to photograph apparitions using movie and still cameras. In addition to stone throwing and other types of object movement, he reported hearing the unexplained sound of ringing bells and unearthed a woman's skeleton from beneath the floor of the basement. When he and his researchers conducted a séance to contact the spirit world, they apparently received a message regarding the dead woman's identity: She was a nun who had been murdered in 1667 by a man who had convinced her to run away with him.

A similar story had already been told to explain the Borley Rectory hauntings. According to legend, the ghost was the spirit of a nun who had tried to run away with a man and was later caught and executed for breaking her vow to the church. She was supposedly buried in the walls of a building that once existed on the site of the rectory. However, there is no record that such a structure ever existed, and the identity of the skeleton has never been determined.

In the end, Price concluded that the apparition and the poltergeist events had two different causes. The ghost was the image of someone who once lived in the house, an image that had been left behind and was somehow being transmitted to the people who visited there. The poltergeist

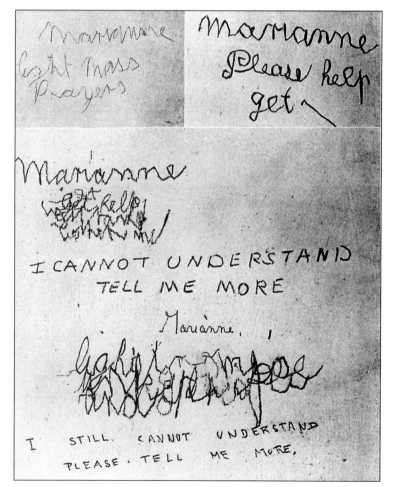

Marianne Foyster's writings on the walls of the Borley Rectory made investigators believe that she was somehow responsible for the poltergeist activity there.

activity was caused by someone living in the house while the activity was taking place, the wife of Reverend Lionel Foyster. During his investigation Price encountered messages addressed to Foyster's wife, Marianne, written on walls. This made him believe that she was somehow responsible for them—along with the fact that when she moved out of the house, the poltergeist aspect of the haunting ended.

However, skeptics subsequently pointed out that the poltergeist activity did not begin until after Price had become involved in the case. Moreover, a few people connected with the case accused Price of faking the poltergeist activity. One person insisted that Price had kept stones in his pocket throughout his time at the rectory, and two people said they had seen Price throwing stones. Even Price's own secretary, Lucy Kaye, noted that the stone throwing never occurred unless Price was present.

The Amityville Horror

Charges of fraud are common in cases of place-associated poltergeist activity, particularly when someone stands to make money off of such activity. A hotel, for example, can increase its number of visitors just by claiming to have its own ghost or poltergeist. Homeowners, too, can become rich because of a poltergeist, as was the case with an incident known as the Amityville Horror.

In 1975 Kathy and George Lutz and their three children moved into a three-story house in Amityville, New York, that had been the site of a gruesome murder the previous year. At first the Lutz family was unconcerned over their house's history, but within a few days they began to experience poltergeist activity that included banging doors and windows and mysterious noises. Then the activity apparently escalated to include physical contact with the experients. Members of the Lutz family claimed to have

been pushed, pinched, and beaten, and Kathy Lutz reported that on one occasion she was levitated off of a bed. In addition, the family said that green slime had dripped from a ceiling and that insects would gather in certain areas of the house for no reason. Just twenty-eight days after moving into the house, they abandoned it. They then called in Ed and Lorraine Warren from Connecticut, who claimed to be able to contact the spirits of the dead. The Warrens conducted a séance and later claimed that the house was indeed possessed by some kind of evil spirit.

This was exactly the claim that a previous occupant of the house had made. Ronald DeFeo Jr., who had murdered his parents and four siblings in the house, pleaded insanity during his trial, insisting that a ghost had forced him to commit the killings. A jury, however, believed the motivation suggested by the prosecutor: that DeFeo simply wanted

Twenty-eight days after moving in, the Lutz family abandoned their house in Amityville, New York, due to alleged poltergeist experiences.

his parents' life insurance money. As a result, DeFeo was convicted on six counts of second-degree murder.

George and Kathy Lutz not only knew this story, but they had discussed it with DeFeo's attorney, William Weber. In 1979 Weber stated that he believed this discussion inspired the Lutzes' to fake their poltergeist experiences in order to profit from them. In fact, he sued for a portion of the money the Lutz family made from their experience. This sum was considerable. Once the Warrens had declared the house haunted, the Lutzes joined with

The Lutzes' story was recorded in a book and film titled The Amityville Horror. *Some people believe, however, that the Amityville Horror was a hoax.*

author Jay Anson to write a "true story" entitled *The Amityville Horror*, which quickly became a best-seller and inspired a 1979 movie by the same name along with a half-dozen sequels. The Warrens worked as consultants on one sequel, *Amityville II*, and made many public appearances to promote the film.

By this time, however, new owners had moved into the house, and they were experiencing absolutely no poltergeist activity. Moreover, they felt that the *Amityville* book and movies were damaging their quality of life by turning their house into a tourist attraction. They sued the book's publisher, author Jay Anson, and the Lutz family, insisting that the Amityville haunting had been a hoax. Other people came forward to support this claim, pointing out inconsistencies in the Lutzes' story. For example, the Lutzes said that after fleeing the house on a particular date, they never went back, but a neighbor revealed that they had held a garage sale there the following day. In addition, several psychic researchers who had investigated the haunting could find no proof that any poltergeist activity had actually taken place there. Eventuallly Weber won his lawsuit, and the new owners received a settlement in exchange for dropping their legal action.

Pranks

Accusations of fraud are not only common when money is involved but also when poltergeist activity centers around teenagers, as it so often does. Skeptics believe that many cases of poltergeist activity are simply pranks perpetrated by clever teens. Such an accusation was made after a noted case of poltergeist activity in 1958 in Seaford, Long Island. In this instance, the poltergeist appeared to be in residence with the family of a twelve-year-old boy named Jimmy Hermann. The spirit produced mysterious noises and sometimes moved objects, but it primarily enjoyed removing bottle tops and lids, whether by popping or unscrewing. Whenever any of these things would happen, Jimmy would be nearby. Many times he was the only one present.

Disturbed by their alleged poltergeist's activities, Jimmy's parents called in two leading experts on the paranormal, Dr. J. G. Pratt and Dr. J. B. Rhine. They saw nothing unusual while in the Hermann house, and could find no cause for the events there other than something paranormal. Hearing this, a magician and skeptic named Milbourne Christopher contacted the Hermanns and asked to examine the house. The family refused his request. Christopher then invited Pratt and several reporters to his home to witness a demonstration related to the Hermann case. Once the group was assembled, Christopher announced that the Hermann house was not haunted at all. Suddenly several lids apparently jumped off of bottles in the next room and several objects appeared to fly across the room.

Christopher then showed the astonished group how he had pulled off these tricks. The flying objects had been set in motion by Christopher, acting while his guests were distracted by the noise of the lids popping off. To make them fly, he had attached them to thin black threads, which he then yanked at the key moment. The sound of the lids had also been created by Christopher. After triggering the sound he abruptly turned his head in the direction of the bottles and his guests simply assumed that the sound had come from them. In actuality, the lids had been off the bottles since before the guests arrived.

But despite Christopher's successful demonstration, Pratt rejected the possibility that Jimmy Hermann could have used such tricks to fake a poltergeist haunting. The expert remained convinced that some kind of paranormal phenomenon was responsible for what happened in Seaford. However, he was unwilling to make a conclusion regarding exactly what type of phenomenon it might be.

Investigation Techniques

Similarly, many people remain convinced that the Borley Rectory haunting was also genuine. No one ever proved that Harry Price had used any kind of trickery to create the poltergeist activity. However, critics of his investigative techniques suggest that he was probably mistaken about much of what he saw. In one instance, for example, he

No one could ever prove that Harry Price, paranormal investigator at the Borley Rectory, was a fraud.

jumped to the conclusion that a hazy area photographed in a room had been a ghost; in fact, though, it was later proved to have been smoke from the fireplace.

Skeptics have also criticized Price for beginning his investigation with a biased opinion. He clearly believed in ghosts before beginning his work; therefore, critics say, his interpretation of the events that followed could not be objective. Price not only approached his investigation with the view that the most likely cause of the haunting was a spirit, but he also included three people on his team of investigators who claimed to be able to communicate with ghosts. Skeptics think that it is nonsense to include ghost communicators, also known as mediums, on a scientific research team, but those who believe in ghosts are convinced that mediums can provide information vital to the study of ghosts and poltergeists.

Chapter 3

Communicating with Spirits

In 1942 New York newspaper columnist Danton Walker moved into a run-down house that had been built before the Revolutionary War and began restoring it to its original condition. The grounds of the estate were very near the site of a well-known Revolutionary War battle, the Battle of Stony Point (1779), and had been used as the headquarters for General Anthony Wayne of the Continental army. Many historians believe that the house itself was used to store arms, ammunition, and food for soldiers as well as to imprison captured enemy soldiers.

The house was also reputed to be haunted. One woman who had lived there insisted that she had often seen the apparition of an old man and heard knocking throughout the house, but her fears were dismissed as nonsense. Nonetheless, Walker soon believed them to be valid. After he moved into the house, he often felt as though someone were watching him, and after a little over a year there he began to hear odd noises. Others, too, began to experience odd phenomena. According

Danton Walker was convinced that his Revolutionary War–era home was haunted.

to ghost expert Hans Holzer, who discussed the case with Walker,

> Mr. Walker's butler, Johnny, remarked to his employer that the house was a nice place to stay in "if they would let you alone." Questioning revealed that Johnny, spending the night in the house alone, had gone downstairs three times during the night to answer knocks at the front door. An Italian workman named Pietro, who did some repairs on the house, reported sounds of someone walking up the stairs in midafternoon "with heavy boots on," at a time when there definitely was no one else in the place. Two occasional guests of the owner also were disturbed, while reading in the living room, by the sound of heavy footsteps overhead.[12]

There was also physical evidence that something unusual was happening. Though no one visiting the house saw a ghost, they did see pictures fall off walls, and objects in the house often broke under mysterious conditions. In addition, certain areas in the house would grow inexplicably cold, and lights would blink on and off for no apparent reason. One guest also felt an invisible hand slap his face in the middle of the night.

A Rescue Circle

Holzer noticed that all of the ghost stories related to Walker's house had a common theme: "Playing pranks, puzzling people, or even frightening them, were not part of the ghost's purpose; they were merely his desperate devices for getting attention, attention for something he very much wanted to say."[13] Consequently, Holzer suggested that a "rescue circle" be held—a gathering of people who would attempt to communicate with the ghost and find out why it was haunting the house. In

November 1952 Holzer went to the house with a group of experts in the paranormal that included a prominent medium, Eileen Garrett.

A medium is a person who claims the ability to communicate with spirits on behalf of other people. In other words, a medium acts as the "go-between" by which the living can talk to the dead. Mediums effect this communication by various means; in Garrett's case, she put herself into an altered state of consciousness, much like deep meditation, known as a hypnotic trance. Then, according to Holzer,

> Quite suddenly her own personality vanished, and the medium sank back into her chair completely lifeless, very much like an unused garment discarded for the time being by its owner. But not for long. A few

A medium, like the man shown here (with the young woman behind him), is a person who claims to be able to communicate with ghosts.

seconds later, another personality "got into" the medium's body, precisely the way one dons a shirt or coat.[14]

The spirit that took over Garrett's body was supposedly one of her "spirit guides." Many mediums claim to have one or more of these spirits, who act as liaisons between the medium and the rest of the spirit world. In the Walker case, Garrett's guide was an East Indian man named Uvani. To observers, it seemed as though Uvani was inside Garrett's body, speaking through her, and Garrett's demeanor changed when Uvani "possessed" her. As Holzer relates,

As "he" sat up . . . it was obvious that we had before us a gentleman from India. Facial expression, eyes, color of skin, movements, the folded arms, and the finger movements that accompanied many of his words were all those of a native of India. As Uvani addressed us, he spoke in perfect English, except for a faltering word now and then or an occasional failure of idiom, but his accent was typical.[15]

This spirit then told observers that he was in contact with the spirit that was haunting Walker's house and would allow it to take control of Garrett's body. Suddenly, Garrett fell to the floor, moaned in pain, and began speaking in broken English. Haltingly, in response to a series of questions, this spirit gave his name as Andrewski and told the story of how he had been tortured to death in Walker's house during the Revolutionary War. He said that soldiers had been trying to make him tell where he had hidden some plans, which were buried just to the east of the house. Additionally, he said that Walker resembled his dead brother Hans, who had also been killed during the war. After referring to Hans, the ghost seemed to utter a Polish exclamation, "*Jilitze.*"

The Haunting Ends

When Andrewski was done communicating, Uvani appeared to resume control of Garrett and talk about the spirit who had just "left":

> It would appear that he is from time to time like one in a coma—he wakes, dreams, and loses himself again, and I gather from the story that he is not always aware of people. Sometimes he says it is a long dream. . . . He has a very strong feeling that [Walker is] like his brother. . . . This may account for his desire to be near [him].[16]

Uvani then said that he would escort Andrewski to the spirit world, providing those in the rescue circle said a prayer. Once this was done, the ghost did indeed appear to stop haunting Walker's house. No other paranormal events occurred there.

Eileen Garrett was a prominent trance medium during the mid-twentieth century.

However, none of Andrewski's story could be confirmed later. Although records show that there were several Revolutionary War soldiers named Andreas, a name that would have been the Americanized version of Andrewski, none seems to fit the profile of Walker's spirit. However, Holzer does not find this unusual because records from the era are incomplete. Moreover, while looking for proof that Hans could have existed, he did find one fact that might corroborate Andrewski's story:

Margaret (left) and Catherine Fox (middle) admitted that their communications with the spirit world were fake.

the Slavic exclamation '*Jilitze . . . Jilitze . . .*' which the ghost made during the interrogation might have been 'Ulica . . . Ulica . . .' I found that a Johannes Ulick (Hans Ulick could be spelled that way) did indeed serve in 1779 in the Second Tryon County Regiment."[17]

People who believe that Garrett really did contact a spirit argue that this fact is highly significant. Skeptics counter that it is a misguided effort to create proof where there is none. They also point out that no buried documents were ever found near Walker's house, suggesting that Garrett's trance was fake and no spirit ever controlled her.

The Fox Sisters

This lack of faith in Eileen Garrett's ability is particularly understandable when one considers that the first spirit communicators to be called mediums admitted to being fakes. They were Kate and Margaret Fox, who were both under the age of sixteen. (Records vary as to their precise age.) In 1847 or 1848 (again, records vary) their family began to hear unexplained noises in a house they had recently occupied. At least two previous occupants had heard similar noises. But this time there was a new twist to the mysterious phenomenon. When the girls knocked on a table, an unseen hand knocked back. When they asked the spirit questions, telling it that rapping three times meant "yes" and no raps meant "no," it answered them. When they recited the alphabet, it knocked whenever they were meant to write down a letter, thereby spelling out words.

Over a series of days, the Fox sisters acted as mediums for their family and neighbors, who questioned the spirit and determined that in life it had been a traveling salesman who had been murdered and buried in the Fox family's cellar. The townspeople then dug up the cellar, and by some accounts they did indeed find human bones. However, since much about the early years of the Fox mediums involves rumor and hearsay, this is doubtful. In addition, the former owner of the house, John Bill, denied ever murdering anyone. Although he remained under suspicion for quite some time, he was never officially charged with a crime.

Meanwhile, crowds continued to gather to watch the Fox sisters perform, and in late 1849 they appeared in an auditorium before a large paying audience. This was the first of many such appearances across the country. The Fox sisters also held private spirit-contacting sessions, which they called sittings. Today's word for similar spirit-contacting sessions, *séance*, is the French word for *sitting*.

During séances, the Fox sisters popped their toe and finger joints to fool people into believing that spirits were communicating with them.

By the time the Fox sisters began conducting private sittings, they were claiming the ability to contact not just one spirit but almost any spirit. In their sessions, clients would ask them to contact the spirit of a particular loved one, and they would comply. This marked the birth of the spiritualist movement, which lasted until the early twentieth century. During this time, hundreds of professional mediums established themselves in the United States and Europe, and thousands of people visited them attempting to contact dead relatives.

The Fox sisters later confessed that they were fakes. At a public demonstration in 1888, they showed exactly how they had produced the rapping noises by popping their toe and finger joints.

Physical Versus Mental Mediums

From the outset, mediums could be divided into two categories: physical mediums and mental mediums. Physical mediums were by far the most prevalent during the spiritualist movement. Much like modern magicians, they typically performed on dimly lit stages, astounding audiences with physical proof that ghosts were actually present. Objects would suddenly and mysteriously appear on stage and just as mysteriously disappear again. A blaring trumpet, for example, might be seen floating behind the medium, and a substance called ectoplasm— a glowing green gel that the medium said was the basic material of which ghosts were made—might appear to ooze from the medium's mouth, nose, ears, or pores.

Even when physical mediums performed in private, they would amaze audiences with a variety of tricks. Rapping sounds were just one type of physical proof that spirits were present. Another was called direct writing, and was the spontaneous and unexplained appearance of handwriting that appeared to belong to the ghost. The medium would cover a slate, and when it was later uncovered, there would be a handwritten message on it.

The first physical medium associated with this trick was Henry Slade, who was eventually caught with a tiny piece of chalk hidden between his toes. Although he denied its connection to his spirit writings, his credibility was damaged. Many other physical mediums of the era were also exposed as frauds.

From this point on, people were suspicious of physical mediums. However, they did not stop believing that spirit communication was possible. Instead, they decided that mental mediums—which include people like Eileen Garrett—were more reliable, and among people who believe in ghosts that bias remains today.

Unlike physical mediums, mental mediums do not try to produce objects and sounds that seem to prove the existence of spirits as entities separate from themselves. Proof that a spirit is present comes instead from information that the spirit provides while communicating with the medium—information that could not have been known by the medium prior to the communication. In addition, whereas physical mediums have traditionally performed in front of large audiences, most mental mediums work privately, either with just one person or with a small group.

During the heyday of the Fox sisters, small-group séances gradually became a popular social event. Called a home circle, this event traditionally takes place in a private home, but not always the home of the medium. In fact, sometimes a professional medium is not involved at all; amateurs might lead the séance instead. In either case, no

Although he always professed his innocence, Henry Slade was the first physical medium to be exposed as a fraud.

fee is charged to the guests who are invited to participate in the home circle, but donations are always accepted when a professional medium is present.

To perform the séance, the medium requires participants to sit around a table holding hands in a dimly lit room. The medium then calls out to the spirits, expecting an answer. If the medium is a physical one, this answer comes via rapping, as with the Fox sisters, or direct writing, as with Henry Slade. For mental mediums, however, the answer is generally transmitted through direct-voice communication or automatic writing.

Automatic Writing

With automatic writing, the spirit apparently takes control of the medium's hand and uses it to write messages. Automatic writing takes place with the medium in a trance, but it can also be triggered by hypnosis in people who are not involved in spirit communication. In his book *The Unexplained!*, Allen Spraggett reports that

> trance writing is not, of itself, a paranormal phenomenon, but merely a form of unconscious activity, on a par with sleep walking, only more complex. Hypnosis can be used to induce automatic writing, either during the actual trance or in the form of a post-hypnotic suggestion. Therapists can use such automatic writing (or drawing) to enable the patient to exteriorize subconscious problems that he cannot verbalize, or dredge up material otherwise shrouded in total amnesia.[18]

As an example of nonparanormal automatic writing, Spraggett tells of one man who sought psychiatric help because he was a compulsive hand washer. Under hypnosis, he wrote an account of a beating his father gave him because his hands were dirty. Prior to the hypnosis, the man had not recalled this incident at all. Afterward, he was

This Italian mental medium, although right-handed, holds a pen in her left hand and writes automatically, revealing messages she is said to be unaware of.

amazed at what he had written down and had no memory of performing the task.

Because of its use in psychiatry, automatic writing is only considered paranormal if the person doing the writing is recounting facts that he or she could not possibly know. One famous example of this occurred in 1913, when Mrs. Joseph Curran wrote novels, poetry, and proverbs that were supposedly the words of Patience Worth, the spirit of an English maid who died in 1649. Worth's collected works were written in seventeenth-century dialect and showed a knowledge of Elizabethan England that Mrs. Curran did not possess. Therefore, although some people called Curran a fraud, Spraggett says that

> the suggestion that Mrs. Curran was a fraud who secretly crammed in libraries does not wash. How much cramming can a person do? Besides, this would not explain Patience's remarkable writing talent. If Mrs. Curran had such talent why should she resort to an artifice such as the ghostly Miss Worth to express it? . . . Of course, it is possible that Mrs. Curran was a . . . literary genius who could . . . express this hidden potential only through the secondary self called Patience Worth. . . . [However, Patience herself] was positively insulting in her assessment of Mrs. Curran's intelligence, or lack of it.[19]

Interestingly, in writing down Worth's words, Curran did not seem to be in a trance. She also did not use a pen or pencil but rather a device known as a Ouija board.

Ouija Boards

Invented in the late 1800s, the Ouija board has letters, numbers, and "yes" and "no" printed on it. The name *Ouija* refers to these symbols; *oui* and *ja* mean "yes" in French and German, respectively. To use the board, the medium puts two hands lightly on a planchette, which is a small teardrop-shaped platform that functions as a pointer while resting on the board. The medium then asks the spirit to move the planchette to spell out words.

Since 1966 the Ouija board has been sold as a game by the Parker Brothers Company, but it is still considered by many to be a serious means of spirit communication. In fact, some people involved in paranormal activities warn that the device can be dangerous. For example, Hans Holzer says, "using a board can bring trouble if those using

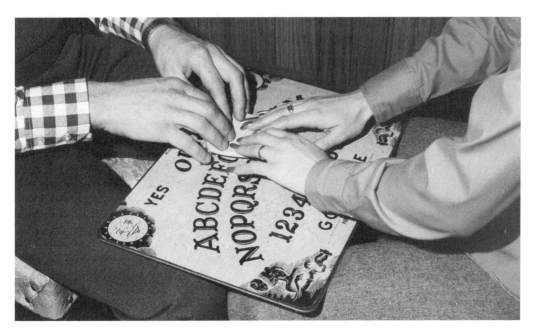

it are potential deep-trance mediums, because an unscrupulous person on the other side [i.e., the spirit world] might want to come in and take over the players, which would result in possession."[20] Similarly, in a guidebook to ghosts, magician Tom Ogden states, "The real danger . . . [in using a Ouija board] comes when a neophyte [beginner] asks a spirit to provide physical proof of its existence. This request may 'open a doorway,' allowing a violent or physically destructive spirit to enter the material world."[21]

In fact, in some cases the neophyte triggers a haunting without even making such a request. This was apparently the case in a haunting in Kansas City, Kansas, that was investigated by Hans Holzer. In his book *Ghosts*, he reports that in 1964 a forty-nine-year-old housewife, "Mrs. G.," was invited to attend a spiritualist church, and while there she heard members discussing how to contact spirits with a Ouija board. She decided to buy a board and try it herself. Prior to this time, Mrs. G. had experienced two paranormal phenomena. Often she would know what someone would say before they said it, and on one occasion she saw an

The Ouija board has been sold as a game since 1966, but paranormal researchers warn against using it as a toy.

apparition of a man when she awoke in the middle of the night, although at the time she had dismissed it as a dream.

When Mrs. G. put her hands on the planchette, a very strange thing happened. She felt it vibrate, and the longer she left her hands on the planchette, the stronger the vibration became. Then her hands began to move the planchette, seemingly against her will. It pointed to a series of letters that spelled out, "Hello, this is John W."[22] Mrs. G. was shocked. John W. was a man who had been in love with her and gotten upset when she married someone else. He had recently died of a heart attack.

Now the board continued to spell out words, apparently from John W., saying that he still loved Mrs. G. and wanted to be with her always. The spirit also complained about the way she had once spurned him. Upset, Mrs. G. put the board away, but soon she found herself drawn to it again. Day after day she would communicate with John W. Then one day she was startled to hear the sound of John W.'s voice, speaking directly to her within her mind. From this point on, he never stopped talking to her. Moreover, she began to feel as though he were right next to her. As Holzer reports,

> She threw away the accursed Ouija board that had opened the floodgates to the invasion from the beyond. But it did not help much. He was there, always present, and he could communicate with her through her own psychic sense. She found it difficult to fall asleep. About that time she noticed that she was no longer alone in bed. . . . [After he tried to kiss her] she fought off his advances as best she could, but it did not deter him in the least. . . . [Now] nothing mattered in her life but to rid herself of this nightmare and return to the placid life she had been leading prior to the incident with the Ouija board.[23]

Finally Mrs. G. went to a physician for help, and when he could find nothing physically wrong with her, she visited a hypnotist. Once she was in a hypnotic trance, Mrs. G. began speaking in the voice of the spirit, and the hypnotist was able to carry on a conversation with "John W." During this conversation, the spirit said that it would never leave Mrs. G., and indeed it never did. However, over the ensuing years Mrs. G. learned to ignore John W.'s comments, and his visits with her lessened.

Skeptics would suggest that Mrs. G.'s experience was the result of a psychological problem, not a spirit problem. However, sometimes the Ouija board has appeared to provide physical evidence that a ghost is present. For example, Tom Ogden reports,

> Katy D., a family friend, tells about a time she stayed overnight at her grandmother's and decided to play with a Ouija board. She tried to contact her late grandfather and asked for a sign of his presence. At first, she was disappointed. The only word that the planchette spelled out was "candles." . . . The next morning, Katy awoke to find all four candles [in her room] burning brightly. Her grandmother hadn't lit them. Had the grandfather told Katy through the Ouija board the night before that he'd use the candles to give her a sign?[24]

But even when Ouija boards are associated with physical manifestations, skeptics believe that the event is caused by the individual using the board rather than by a ghost. In Katy's case, for example, they would suggest that her subconscious mind moved the planchette and that she lit the candles herself during the night but retained no memory of doing so.

Direct-Voice Communication

The same argument—that the medium's subconscious mind is creating the phenomenon—has been applied to the other common means by which spirits appear to communicate, direct-voice communication. This was the technique

Here, people gather to watch a medium channel the spirit of John the Baptist. Since the 1970s, several people have come forward and claimed to be channelers.

Eileen Garrett used to investigate Walker's house. With direct-voice communication, the spirit can appear to talk through the medium, using the medium's vocal cords, but in a voice that sounds different from the medium's normal one. In addition, the spirit's voice may seem to come from a spot just beside the medium, and the medium's mouth does not appear to move. In such cases skeptics believe that the medium is using a trick called ventriloquism, whereby a person can make it appear that his or her voice is coming from a different location.

When the spirit uses the medium's vocal cords while seeming to take possession of his or her body, it is called channeling. This term was first used in the 1970s, and since then several people have claimed to be channelers. One of the most famous is J. Z. Knight, who claims that her body is often taken over by the spirit of Ramtha, a thirty-five-thousand-year-old warrior from the lost city of

Atlantis. Ramtha makes predictions about the future, but they are vague. Nonetheless, thousands of people pay hundreds of dollars to attend Knight's seminars, and she currently has her own school, the Ramtha School of Enlightenment, which attracts three thousand students for each half-year session.

In the late 1980s, magician and skeptic James Randi attempted to prove that supporters of people like Knight

James Randi is a skeptic and magician who has proved thousands of paranormal claims to be fake.

are misguided. Randi has debunked thousands of claims related to paranormal phenomena, and to discredit channelers he devised an elaborate hoax. He taught a young man named Jose Alvarez to act like a channeler and, through a variety of ruses, convinced the Australian media that Alvarez was a famous South American channeler whose body was often taken over by "Carlos," a two-thousand-year-old spirit from Venezuela. After the media reported on Alvarez's amazing ability, people flocked to his public appearances. They also accepted his intentionally meaningless advice and predictions as valuable, and they offered to pay thousands of dollars for some crystals he claimed would heal vague aches and pains.

Even more surprisingly, after the hoax was revealed, many of these people continued to express belief in "Carlos." In an interview with television reporter John Stossel, Jose Alvarez said, "At the end, there were people saying, 'We know everything they're saying about you. We don't care. We believe in you.'"[25] James Randi added, "No amount of evidence, no matter how good it is or how much there is of it, is ever going to convince the true believer to the contrary."[26]

But some people would say the same thing about skeptics—that no amount of proof would convince them to believe in the paranormal. Nonetheless, many believers have tried to devise investigations that will convince skeptics that ghosts really are spirits of the dead. Meanwhile, some skeptics have dedicated their lives to discrediting mediums, and several scientists have attempted to investigate ghost stories with some neutrality.

Chapter 4

Investigating Hauntings

A typical example of a modern investigation into a haunting took place in 1977 at a haunted house in Enfield, England. It was not an old manor home but a relatively modern, modest house belonging to the Harper family, which consisted of a mother and her four children ages seven to thirteen. One evening they began hearing unexplained knocking and scratching noises. They called the police, and the officers heard the noises too, but after a thorough search of the house no cause could be found. The next day they saw small objects, such as marbles and building blocks, rise and fly through the air of their own accord.

Deciding that evil spirits were at work, the Harpers asked a priest to bless the house. When that failed to end the poltergeist activity, they asked a medium to contact the spirit and ask that it stop haunting them. The medium was unable to communicate with the entity, although she did detect some kind of disturbance in the house. The poltergeist activity continued, and when a newspaper reporter and a photographer showed up to do a story on the house after a neighbor called them, they were pelted with flying objects. Reported in many newspapers, this incident made the house famous.

At this point the Society of Psychical Research (SPR) became involved. The oldest paranormal research organization

Paranormal investigator Maurice Grosse stands near some of the smaller items from the Enfield case.

still in existence today, it routinely sends investigators to sites of unusual events throughout the world. The first investigator the SPR sent to Enfield was Maurice Grosse, an inexperienced trainee. After he, too, was pelted with objects, it became clear that he could not handle the study alone and a more experienced SPR investigator, Guy Playfair, went to work on the case as well. Also involved was SPR photographer Graham Morris.

Together these three men spent a year working on the case. During that time they noted over two thousand unusual incidents, including flying marbles that landed on the floor but did not roll, books that appeared to change direction ninety degrees while flying through the air, and heavy furniture that moved while they were watching. They tried to document these incidents with photographic equipment and tape recorders but failed. In his book *Paranormal People*, Paul Chambers explains why:

Many attempts were made to photograph the phenomena and record them on tape, but, as Playfair says, the poltergeist seemed to be a bit camera-shy. Things would either occur outside the range of the equipment or the equipment would mysteriously malfunction at crucial times. Morris found that his camera flashes would drain themselves, even after being recharged, and both Grosse and Playfair had numerous problems with their audio tape recorders, including parts of the machinery bending themselves while inside the casing.[27]

Skeptics find such mishaps too convenient, suggesting that the researchers were trying to hide the fact that there had actually been nothing unusual to photograph. However, many people witnessed the poltergeist activity in the Harpers' house and shared the researchers' frustration at being unable to photograph it.

Devising Tests

But Playfair and Grosse did not just act as observers in the house. They also devised experiments to test various theories regarding the origin of the poltergeist activities. Their first assumption was that the Harper children were simply playing a prank on them. Therefore, they watched the youngsters carefully and at certain times during the investigation

Guy Playfair (shown here) helped devise experiments and tests to uncover the source of the Harper poltergeist. No irrefutable cause was ever discovered.

sent them out of the house. Still the strange events occurred, and the investigators could find no evidence that the children were involved in any mischief.

Their next assumption was that the poltergeist activity was somehow created by eleven-year-old Janet, who seemed to be the focus of much of the activity. She was usually present whenever a strange incident occurred, and as the research project continued she seemed to be tormented by unseen hands that pinched and hit her. To test whether Janet was manipulating her environment through sleight of hand, the researchers tried restraining her, but the incidents still occurred.

The investigators also made careful note of events that did not seem connected to Janet. On one such occasion, Playfair and Grosse were experimenting with spirit communication while

Janet was absent from the house. They had gotten the spirit to knock once for "yes" and twice for "no" while they asked it questions. The questioning session had just gotten started when Playfair asked, "Do you realize that you are dead?" Paul Chambers reports on what happened next:

> After that all hell broke loose in the house, with one upstairs room being totally ransacked. No further communications were made in this manner between Playfair and the poltergeist. Grosse, however, had more success and through the rapping code managed to establish that the entity had lived in the house for 30 years but had left 53 years before. Eventually the knocking became nonsensical and Grosse asked, 'Are you having a game with me?' A couple of seconds later he was struck on the head by a box full of cushions.[28]

However, Janet remained the primary focus of the poltergeist's anger. It threw things at her, appeared to try to suffocate her with a cushion, and wrote obscene things about her on the walls. Eventually it also seemed to possess her body on occasion, using direct-voice communication to curse the investigators. At these times Janet would behave much like a medium, losing control of her body, speaking in an altered voice, and claiming to be the ghost of first one man and then another. However, unlike a medium, she would only talk when no one was in the room with her, shouting her words through a closed door. When she was sent to the hospital for tests, the poltergeist began focusing on one of her two younger brothers, pinching and hitting him instead. As with the rapping incident, this would suggest that the poltergeist was an entity separate from Janet.

Unknown Causes

After a year of in-depth study, the investigators could not come up with an indisputable explanation for the Harpers' troubles. Nonetheless, during the latter part of 1978 the

Most of the poltergeist activity in the Harper case centered around eleven-year-old Janet (shown here with her mother).

poltergeist activity diminished and finally stopped altogether. Two years later Playfair's book on the case, *This House is Haunted!*, was published and immediately became a best-seller. This brought the Harpers' experience to the attention of other researchers, and in 1982 physicist J. Hasted decided to see whether Janet had any paranormal ability. He attached her to a machine that could measure her weight electronically with great precision, then asked her to make herself lighter. Over a period of thirty seconds, the measurement dropped one kilogram.

Hasted theorized that Janet was either levitating herself imperceptibly in order to reduce her weight or using psychokinesis (PK) to alter the scale's measurement mechanism. Since PK has widely been theorized to cause poltergeist activity, this finding could be significant, although as skeptics point out, there is no proof that PK even exists and no evidence that Janet was in fact using it.

The Harper investigation illustrates a common problem with paranormal research. Even after an exhaustive study, in which many theories are carefully explored and rejected, it is difficult for believers in ghosts to come up with data that skeptics will accept as valid. Moreover, even if all the phenomena associated with a particular haunting are observable by investigators working under controlled conditions—that is, all events can be proven not to be the product of fraud or hallucination—there are other explanations for the phenomena other than that a ghost is causing them. Part of the investigator's job is to eliminate as many of these other explanations as possible.

Some experts suggest that mediums and channelers may in fact just be people afflicted with multiple personality disorder, a condition brought on by severe childhood abuse.

Multiple Personality Disorders

One example of alternative explanations for paranormal activity is multiple personality disorder. With this disorder,

the afflicted person develops additional personalities, as if his or her original personality had split into many. When one of these personalities is in control of the individual, the other personalities, which are relegated to a trancelike state, might later retain no knowledge of what happened during that period.

Most cases of multiple personality disorder, also called split personality disorder, have been brought on by severe child abuse that causes the original personality to "go away" and another to step in to cope with the situation. Some experts on the paranormal have suggested that this disorder can occur even without childhood trauma and might explain why mediums seem able to contact spirits. For instance, Allen Spraggett says that the fact that multiple personality disorders have been proven to be a real psychological phenomenon indicates

> that a spirit control is not necessarily supernormal but may be merely abnormal, a secondary personality of the medium. This would not, of course, imply play-acting or faking by the medium. A secondary personality is not a conscious impersonation, but an autonomous self with a psychic life of its own—another "person" occupying the same body as the normal person.[29]

Like mediums, people afflicted with multiple personality disorders change in demeanor when they "become" an alternate personality. However, the basic facts about their bodies—blood chemistry, heart pressure, nerve reflexes, and so forth—remain the same. Consequently, heart disease specialist Dr. Cornelius Horace Traeger decided that one could determine whether a medium was really being possessed by a separate entity simply by taking laboratory readings of various body characteristics both before and after the "spirit possessions." In 1965 he asked Eileen Garrett to participate in his study, and she agreed.

Eileen Garrett (shown here in 1926) participated in a 1965 medical study to refute her paranormal abilities. Shocked and confused doctors were unable to prove her a fake.

Traeger tested Garrett both in her normal state and while she was in a twenty-minute trance and under the control of her spirit Uvani, who had apparently agreed to cooperate with the test. Another spirit guide, Abdul Latif, was also involved; he agreed to "enter" Garrett immediately after Uvani "left" and remain in control for twenty minutes. Throughout the experiment, Traeger's tests included measurements of blood count, bleeding time, blood-clotting time, respiration, pulse, heart pressure, heart rate, and Garrett's reaction to various drugs that were administered by injection.

Traeger's test results were so surprising that, according to Allen Spraggett, he was afraid that his colleagues would think he had made some mistake. As Spraggett reports,

When the bleeding time was tested, it was found that in the case of Mrs. Garrett it took three minutes for the bleeding to stop. In Abdul Latif's case, the time was ninety seconds; in that of Uvani, it was only thirty-three seconds. The blood counts—the percentage of white to red corpuscles in a given measure of blood—also varied. For Mrs. Garrett the count was 70, for Uvani 85, and for Abdul Latif 115. These results suggested an actual change in the physical composition of the medium's blood when she was entranced. And in Abdul Latif's case, a test for blood sugar showed such an abnormally high level that the natural diagnosis was diabetes. Yet, in the conscious state, Mrs. Garrett's blood sugar was normal.[30]

Spraggett further reports that the drugs administered to Garrett in various states also showed marked differences. Adrenaline, for example, failed to stimulate Garrett in her normal state because she had a high tolerance for it. But when she was "possessed" by Uvani or Abdul Latif, the drug did stimulate her. Similar variations were found with several other drugs. Her heart rate was also different depending on which entity was being evaluated.

Hypnosis

Spraggett believes that this study provides strong scientific evidence that Eileen Garrett is a genuine medium whose body can be taken over by a being independent of herself. At the same time, he does not believe that this proof is incontrovertible because hypnosis could account for the same changes. Just as people under hypnosis can produce automatic writing that they are later unable to remember, so, too, can physiological changes take place. Spraggett explains:

> It is, for instance, a fact that the secretion of certain enzymes that are normally present only during digestion, such as pepsin, can be induced in a hypnotic subject by the suggestion that he is eating a meal. Also the flow of gastric juices can be stepped up or slowed down by suggestion. . . . [And] we know that a hypnotized subject can become intoxicated by water if he is told it is whiskey. . . . It is conceivable then that the results of the medical tests on Mrs. Garrett and her controls are explainable in terms of self-hypnosis, or identification. . . . Mrs. Garrett may identify so completely with Uvani and Abdul Latif, respectively, that in trance she takes on not only their fancied mannerisms but their physical [characteristics] too—including sugar in the blood and a cardiograph variation.[31]

Interestingly, not only did Garrett use autohypnosis at the beginning of each spirit communication session, but throughout her life she was concerned that her ability to speak to spirits was actually caused by a multiple personality disorder. It was in an attempt to prove her fears false that she volunteered to be tested, not only by Traeger but by other experts as well. She also founded her own research institution, the Parapsychology Foundation, to investigate mediums like herself, and she worked with the Society of Psychical Research (SPR) to expose fraudulent mediums as part of its serious research into paranormal phenomena.

Daniel Home

The SPR was founded in 1873 with the goal of applying scientific methods to the study of paranormal phenomena, after an incident involving medium Daniel Dunglas Home (pronounced "Hume"). Throughout his life Home was associated with paranormal phenomena. When he was a child, his family experienced poltergeist activity that primarily involved unexplained knocking and the displacement of objects. As an adult, Home began holding séances during which he would produce spirit writings, play musical instruments without seeming to touch them, cause objects to materialize, and levitate furniture and people, including himself. Sometimes he levitated spontaneously when no séance was being conducted. When observers would try to pull him back down, they, too, would be raised in the air.

Sir William Crookes, a respected chemist of the time, studied Home as part of an 1869–1875 investigation of mediums and declared him genuine. But when he published a scientific paper about Home in 1871, he was ridiculed by the rest of the scientific community. Consequently, two professors, Henry Sidgwick and Frederick Myers, decided that an organization was needed to support serious studies like the one Crookes conducted, and they established the SPR.

An investigation into medium Daniel Home led to the founding of the Society of Psychical Research (SPR).

Throughout its history, the SPR has tried to approach its research objectively. Sometimes this results in a particular medium being exposed as a fraud. Daniel Home, however, was never proven to be a fraud. Despite the fact that Crookes tested him under controlled laboratory conditions, no explanation could be found for his abilities. Even today many people believe Home to be one of the few genuine physical mediums in history.

More importantly, unlike any other physical medium during the spiritualist movement, Home performed in daylight in front of many witnesses and no one was ever able to duplicate his feats or determine what might have caused them other than the supernatural. Paul Chambers, in his book *Paranormal People*, says,

> One of [Home's] most remarkable achievements was never to be formally found faking his paranormal feats. In an age when people were making a living from debunking [discrediting] famous mediums, he managed to be observed by hundreds of people (some of them eminent scientists) in well-lit conditions and yet was still never caught cheating. Many of those who did accuse him of cheating only did so some time after having been at one of his séances. These accusations occasionally followed the ridiculing of an individual who had initially testified to the validity of some phenomenon. . . . Many explanations have been put forward as to how Home could have faked his phenomena, but most are so complicated as to be impossible when it is borne in mind that Home often performed in lighted conditions in houses where he had never previously been. . . . Scientific studies of Home seem only to have re-enforced the validity of his claims to supernatural powers.[32]

Harry Houdini

One of the debunkers who tried to discredit Home was famous magician Harry Houdini. Houdini believed that it might really be possible to communicate with ghosts, and throughout his life he continued to hope that while exposing false mediums he might find a genuine one. Meanwhile, he grew angry over just how many frauds there were. After witnessing Home's phenomena, Houdini insisted that the man was a charlatan, and he promised that he would be able to prove this by performing the same tricks himself on stage. However, he was never able to do so.

One fraud whom Houdini did expose was Minna Crandon, a Boston surgeon's wife who went by the name of Margery while working as a medium. Considered one of the top physical mediums of her time, in 1924 she asked to be evaluated by a panel of experts as part of a challenge by *Scientific American* magazine. The magazine had promised five thousand dollars to any medium proved to have a real ability to contact spirits. Harry

Here, Harry Houdini tests his "fraud-proof" box on Margery Crandon. Houdini proved conclusively that Crandon was a fake.

Houdini was on the magazine's expert panel, and when he watched Crandon perform, he knew that she was moving objects in her spirit room via devices worked with her feet. He constructed a device that would keep her from moving her feet during a séance, but once the séance was underway, Crandon "accidentally" broke it. Then she—or rather, apparently, her spirit guide, "Walter"—berated Houdini and refused to continue the test.

But although Houdini thought he had definitively proved Crandon a fraud, many people refused to believe him. In fact, Crandon's supporters continued to have faith in her even after she displayed "Walter's" fingerprints and someone discovered they were actually the prints of her dentist.

Searching for Explanations

Daniel Home remained a medium until his retirement in 1873 and died of tuberculosis in 1886. In the years since then, many people have tried to explain his abilities, including James Randi. Randi believes that he has successfully proven Home a fraud, but Paul Chambers reports that

> James Randi maintains that Home was caught cheating on a number of occasions, but he does not list his sources. He has, however, put forward some plausible theories concerning some of Home's paranormal feats. For example, he says that when Home was seen playing an accordion inside a steel cage with one or no hands, in fact he really had a miniature mouth-organ hidden inside his mouth. This has been further supported by the fact that Home's accordion never played more than nine notes (the same as one octave from a mouth organ) and by the discovery of a set of miniature mouth organs in Home's possession

after his death. Despite strong evidence like this, it must be said that practical explanations (ones not involving any mass hysteria) of Home's public demonstrations are thin on the ground.[33]

Chambers speculates that Home's abilities might have been caused by the development of an ability to consciously direct poltergeist activity, such as was associated with him as a child. Others have said that he was simply a stage magician more skilled than Houdini. In fact, magician James Randi has suggested that magic tricks are responsible for a great deal of "paranormal" activity. He says that

James Randi (middle) with Steve (left) and Mike Edwards (right). Although the boys claimed to possess psychic powers, Randi proved that they were using conjuring tricks.

when considering any claim related to the paranormal "it is more rational to suspect trickery than to adopt the preposterous alternative,"[34] which is that ghosts are real.

Randi also believes that there has never been a properly designed and conducted scientific investigation that proves the existence of ghosts as a phenomenon not caused by the experient. Moreover, he is skeptical about the validity of theories related to telepathy, ESP (extrasensory perception), and other psychological phenomena. Meanwhile, Hans Holzer suggests that people like Randi are being unreasonable, arguing that there has already been substantial proof that spirits of the dead do communicate with the living:

> To the materialist and the professional skeptic—that is to say, people who do not wish their belief that death is the end of life as we know it to be disturbed—the notion of ghosts is unacceptable. No matter how much evidence is presented to support the reality of the phenomena, these people will argue against it and ascribe it to any of several "natural" causes. Delusion or hallucination must be the explanation, or perhaps a mirage, if not outright trickery. Entire professional groups that deal in the manufacturing of illusions have taken it upon themselves to label anything that defies their ability to reproduce it artificially through trickery or manipulation as false or nonexistent. Especially among photographers and magicians, the notion that ghosts exist has never been popular. But authentic reports of psychic phenomena along ghostly lines keep coming into reputable report centers such as societies for psychic research, or to parapsychologists like myself.[35]

However, Holzer also adds that people must not blindly believe in the paranormal. They must study reports of hauntings and make decisions regarding their validity based on facts rather than emotion. At the same time, they must remain open to all of the evidence, not just the evidence that supports their preconceptions regarding whether haunted houses are real.

Notes

Introduction: Mysterious Sights, Sounds, and Smells

1. Michael Norman and Beth Scott, *Historic Haunted America*. New York: Tor, 1995, pp. 49–50.
2. Jerome Clark, *Unexplained!* Farmington Hills, MI: Visible Ink, 1999, p. xxv.

Chapter One: Ghosts and Apparitions

3. Quoted in Reader's Digest, *Mysteries of the Unexplained*. Pleasantville, NY: Reader's Digest Association, 1982, p. 177.
4. Quoted in Robin Mead, *Haunted Hotels*. Nashville: Rutledge Hill, 1995, p. 140.
5. Quoted in Norman and Scott, *Historical Haunted America*, p. 240.
6. Hans Holzer, *Ghosts: True Encounters with the World Beyond*. New York: Black Dog & Leventhal, 1997, p. 743.
7. James Randi, *Flim-Flam!: Psychics, ESP, Unicorns, and Other Delusions*. Amherst, NY: Prometheus Books, 1982, pp. 294–95.

Chapter Two: Poltergeists

8. H. J. Irwin, *An Introduction to Parapsychology*. Jefferson, NC: McFarland, 1989, pp. 175–76.
9. Quoted in Editors of Time-Life Books, *Hauntings*. New York: Time-Life Books, 1989, p. 55.
10. Irwin, *An Introduction to Parapsychology*, p. 176.
11. A. R. G. Owen, *Can We Explain the Poltergeist?* New York: Garrett, 1964, pp. 12–13.

Chapter Three: Communicating with Spirits

12. Holzer, *Ghosts*, p. 78.
13. Holzer, *Ghosts*, pp. 79–80.
14. Holzer, *Ghosts*, p. 80.
15. Holzer, *Ghosts*, p. 80.
16. Holzer, *Ghosts*, p. 83.
17. Holzer, *Ghosts*, p. 84.
18. Allen Spraggett, *The Unexplained!* New York: New American Library, 1967, pp. 115–16.
19. Spraggett, *The Unexplained!*, p. 122.
20. Hans Holzer, *Ghosts*, p. 27.
21. Tom Ogden, *The Complete Idiot's Guide to Ghosts and Hauntings*. Indianapolis: Alpha Books/Macmillan USA, 1999, p. 91.
22. Holzer, *Ghosts*, p. 620.
23. Holzer, *Ghosts*, pp. 620–21.
24. Ogden, *The Complete Idiot's Guide to Ghosts and Hauntings*, p. 92.
25. Quoted in John Stossel, "The Power of Belief," transcript of ABC Special Report, aired October 6, 1998, and June 3, 1999, p. 13.
26. Quoted in Stossel, "The Power of Belief," pp. 13–14.

Chapter Four: Investigating Hauntings

27. Paul Chambers, *Paranormal People*. London: Blandford, 1998, pp. 39–40.
28. Chambers, *Paranormal People*, p. 40.
29. Spraggett, *The Unexplained!*, p. 67.

30. Spraggett, *The Unexplained!*, p. 69.
31. Spraggett, *The Unexplained!*, pp. 70–71.
32. Chambers, *Paranormal People*, pp. 84–85.
33. Chambers, *Paranormal People*, p. 85.
34. Randi, *Flim-Flam!* p. 3.
35. Holzer, *Ghosts*, p. 24.

For Further Reading

Mary Batten, *The 25 Scariest Hauntings in the World*. Los Angeles: Lowell House, 1996. For readers ages 9 to 12, this book offers 25 stories of haunted houses throughout the world.

W. Haden Blackman, *The Field Guide to North American Hauntings: Everything You Need to Know About Encountering Over 100 Ghosts, Phantoms, and Spectral Entities*. New York: Three Rivers Press, 1998. Blackman lists over 100 haunted sites and provides information about their histories.

Daniel Cohen, *Ghosts in the House*. New York: Apple, 1995. For readers ages 9 to 12, this book features nine stories of supposedly real haunted houses.

Daniel Cohen, *The Phantom Hitchhiker: And Other Unsolved Mysteries*. New York: Kingfisher Books, 1995. For readers 9 to 12, this book features 13 supposedly true ghost stories.

Troy A. Taylor, *The Ghost Hunter's Guidebook*. Alton, IL: Whitechapel Productions, 1999. This book offers information about how to investigate ghosts and haunted houses, explaining techniques used by modern-day ghosthunters.

Works Consulted

Paul Chambers, *Paranormal People*. London: Blandford, 1998. This book offers interesting information about people who have exhibited paranormal abilities such as mediumship.

Jerome Clark, *Unexplained!* Farmington Hills, MI: Visible Ink, 1999. Written by a believer in UFOs, this book offers information about a variety of mysterious phenomena.

Editors of Time-Life Books, *Hauntings*. New York: Time-Life Books, 1989. This book provides an overview of information about haunted houses and ghosts.

Hans Holzer, *Ghosts: True Encounters with the World Beyond*. New York: Black Dog & Leventhal, 1997. This enormous volume is a compilation of accounts from Holzer's work investigating haunted houses.

H. J. Irwin, *An Introduction to Parapsychology*. Jefferson, NC: McFarland, 1989. Irwin, who teaches parapsychology at the University of New England, offers a comprehensive overview of psychic phenomena.

Robin Mead, *Haunted Hotels*. Nashville: Rutledge Hill, 1995. This is a guidebook telling tourists how to find interesting haunted hotels that are still in operation. It also provides stories about hotel hauntings.

Michael Norman and Beth Scott, *Historic Haunted America*. New York: Tor, 1995. This book is a guide to haunted places throughout the United States that are visited by ghosts from America's history rather than ghosts from modern times.

Tom Ogden, *The Complete Idiot's Guide to Ghosts and Hauntings*. Indianapolis: Alpha Books/Macmillan USA, 1999. Magician Tom Ogden provides detailed information related to ghosts and haunted houses while maintaining a lighthearted attitude toward his subject.

A. R. G. Owen, *Can We Explain the Poltergeist?* New York: Garrett, 1964. A noted researcher into paranormal phenomena examines poltergeist activity in great depth.

James Randi, *Flim-Flam!: Psychics, ESP, Unicorns, and Other Delusions*. Amherst, NY: Prometheus Books, 1982. Written by perhaps the most famous skeptic in America, this book casts a critical eye on a variety of phenomena reputed to be caused by the paranormal.

Reader's Digest, *Mysteries of the Unexplained*. Pleasantville, NY: Reader's Digest Association, 1982. This book is a compilation of stories related to a variety of paranormal phenomena, including ghosts and haunted houses.

Allen Spraggett, *The Unexplained!* New York: New American Library, 1967. Parapsychologist Allen Spraggett offers an overview of paranormal phenomena, including the work of mediums.

John Stossel, "The Power of Belief," transcript of ABC Special Report, aired October 6, 1998, and June 3, 1999. This hour-long television program hosted by reporter John Stossel attempted to debunk a variety of claims related to paranormal phenomena.

Index

Picture Credits

Cover photo: Arthur Tilley/FPG
Archive Photos, 27, 44, 49
Bettmann/Corbis, 43, 55, 61
Corbis, 13
Culver Pictures, 19, 54
Mary Evans Picture Library, 17, 71, 72, 79
Fortean Picture Library, 22, 25, 31, 34, 37, 38, 41, 53, 57, 65, 69, 74, 81
Fortean Picture Library/Dr. Elmar Gruber, 51, 59
Fortean Picture Library/Guy Lyon Playfair, 68
Hulton-Deutsch Collection/Corbis, 47, 77
Northwind Picture Archives, 11, 14
Roger Ressmeyer/Corbis, 64
Winchester Mystery House, 9

About The Author

Patricia D. Netzley received a bachelor's degree in English from the University of California at Los Angeles (UCLA). After graduation she worked as an editor at the UCLA Medical Center, where she produced hundreds of medical articles, speeches, and pamphlets.

Netzley became a freelance writer in 1986. She is the author of several books for children and adults, including Lucent Books's *The Curse of King Tut* and *UFOs*. She and her husband, Raymond, live in southern California with their children, Matthew, Sarah, and Jacob.